KU-542-326

PRESENTED TO

Sophie Myring - mccullagh

By

Tara

Date

20:10:12

Praise him, praise him
Everybody praise him –
He is love, he is love;
Praise him, praise him,
Everybody praise him –
God is love, God is love!

Candle PRAYERS for Toddlers

Compiled by Juliet David
Illustrations by Helen Prole

Illustrated by Helen Prole
Compiled by Juliet David
Published in 2008 by Candle Books,
a publishing imprint of Lion Hudson plc
Copyright © 2008 Lion Hudson plc/Tim Dowley Associates

Every effort has been made to trace and contact copyright owners.
We apologise for any inadvertent omissions or errors.

Acknowledgments
The Lord's Prayer (page 6) from Common Worship:
Services and Prayers for the Church of England
(Church House Publishing, 2000) is
copyright © The English Language Liturgical Consultation,
1988 and is reproduced by permission of the publishers.

Distributed in the UK by Marston Book Services Ltd,
PO Box 269, Abingdon, Oxon OX14 4YN
Distributed in the USA by Kregel Publications,
PO Box 2607, Grand Rapids, Michigan 49501

All rights reserved. No part of this publication may be reproduced, stored
in a retrieval system, or transmitted in any form or by any means - for example,
electronic, photocopy, recording - without the prior written permission of the publisher.

Worldwide co-edition produced by Lion Hudson plc,
Wilkinson House, Jordan Hill Road, Oxford OX2 8DR
Tel: +44 (0)1865 302750 Fax: +44 (0)1865 302757
Email: coed@lionhudson.com

ISBN 978 1 85985 679 6

Third printing March 2011 (manufacturer LH01), Singapore

Contents

The Lord's Prayer

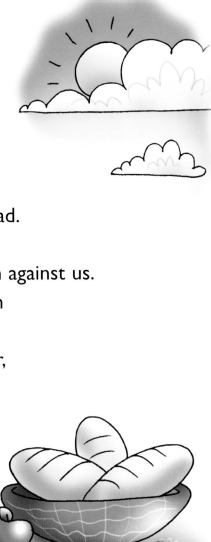

Our Father in heaven,
hallowed be your name,
your kingdom come,
your will be done,
on earth as in heaven.
Give us today our daily bread.
Forgive us our sins
as we forgive those who sin against us.
Lead us not into temptation
but deliver us from evil.
For the kingdom, the power,
and the glory are yours
now and for ever.
Amen.

Good Morning,
Good Morning!

Thank you, God in heaven,
For a day begun.
Thank you for the breezes,
Thank you for the sun.

For this time of gladness,
For our work and play,
Thank you, God in heaven
For another day.

Traditional

Dear God,
Thank you for my friend next door,
And my friend across the street,
And please help me to be a friend
To each and every one I meet.

Anonymous

Dear Lord on high,
Make a clear sky
Make the day fine
And let the sun shine

Traditional

Each morning when I wake, I say,
"Take care of me, dear Lord, today."

Lord Jesus Christ,
be with me today,
And help me
in all I think, or do or say.

Traditional

Loving God, as we start this day,
Make us happy as we play;
Kind and helpful, being fair,
Letting others have their share.

Hi God!

Did you see everything I did today?

- ✓ Got dressed by myself
- ✓ Had cereal for breakfast
- ✓ Cleaned my teeth
- ✓ Went to school
- ✓ Helped teacher
- ✓ Ate my lunch
- ✓ Played in the garden
- ✓ Read a book
- ✓ Played a game
- ✓ Went shopping
- ✓ Rode my tricycle
- ✓ Watched tv
- ✓ Did some drawing
- ✓ Had a bath

What a lot of things I did!

Thank you, God

Mealtimes

Thank you for the world so sweet,
Thank you for the food we eat,
Thank you for the birds that sing,
Thank you, God, for everything.

*To the tune of Twinkle Twinkle Little Star,
by E. Rutter Leatham*

Bless this bunch
as they munch
their lunch.
Amen.

For health and strength
and daily food,
we praise your name,
O Lord.

Traditional

For all we eat, and all we wear,
For daily bread, and nightly care,
we thank you heavenly Father.
Amen.

Good bread, Good meat.
Good Lord, Let's eat!
Amen.

God is great, God is good.
Let us thank him for our food.
By his hands, we are fed.
Let us thank him for our bread.

Traditional, used by US President Jimmy Carter

God bless us (hands on head)
God bless the food (hands around plate)
Amen (hands folded).

Rub a dub dub;
Thanks for the grub;
Yeaaa God!

For every cup and plateful
Lord make us truly grateful.
Amen.

Heavenly Father,
Help the poor people in the world
Who can't just go to the kitchen
and get a biscuit.
Amen.

Tick, Tock,
Hear the clock,
Now it's time to pray.
We fold our hands,
And bow our heads,
And thank the Lord
For our bread today.

We thank you Lord, for happy hearts,
For rain and sunny weather.
Thank you Father for this food
And that we're here together.

Some have meat and cannot eat,
And some want food but lack it.
But we have meat and we can eat
And so the Lord be thanked.

After Robert Burns

Us and this:
God bless.

Quaker grace

Prayer Time

Hush little puppy
  with your bow wow wow,
Hush little kitty
  with your meow, meow, meow.
Hush Mr. Rooster
  with your cock-a-doodle-doo.
Please don't moo-moo, Mrs. Cow.
Hush, hush, hush!
Hush, hush, hush!
Somebody's talking to God right now.

Traditional

My head is still.
My hands are still.
My arms are still.
My feet are still.
Now I put my hands together
to pray.

Anonymous

Father in heaven
hear my prayer.
Keep me in
your love and care.
Amen.

May all the happy things we do
Make you, our Father, happy too.
Amen.

Before we go away,
we bow our heads and pray,
that God will keep us safe and sound
until another day.

Prayer at the end of school day

Lord, teach me to love your children everywhere
Because you are their father –
And mine
Amen.

Lord Jesus,
I think about you sometimes,
even when I'm not praying.

Prayer is
Talking to God,
Listening to God,
Loving God.

Alison Winn

Dear God,
I'm glad you love my brother and sister
and me and everybody.
I want to love you, too,
and grow up to be strong and good.
Amen.

This is the church,
And this is the steeple
Open the doors
And see all the people!
Close the doors
And the people all pray.

(*With hand actions*)

Day by day, dear Lord,
Three things I pray:
To see you more clearly,
To love you more dearly,
To follow you more nearly,
Day by day.

Richard of Chichester (1197-1253)

God, make my life a little light
Within the world to glow;
A little flame that burns so bright
Wherever I may go.

God, make my life a little song
That comforts those who are sad,
That helps others to be strong
And makes the singer glad.

Matilda Betham-Edwards (1836-1919)

Dear God,
Be good to me,
The sea is so wide
And my boat is so small.

Prayer of Breton fishermen

Today!

Dear Lord Jesus,
We have this day only once.
Before it goes,
help us to do the good we can
so it isn't wasted.
Amen.

Dear Jesus,
Please help me at school.
Sometimes I find it hard,
and then I specially need you to help.
Amen.

Keep my little tongue today,
Make it kind while I play;
Keep my hands from doing wrong,
Guide my feet the whole day long.
Amen.

Yesterday I promised
I'd try to be good today.
Lord, please help me keep my promise.

Little deeds of kindness,
Little words of love,
Help to make earth happy,
Like the heaven above.

Julia Carney (1824-1908)

Me, Myself and I

Jesus loves me! – this I know
For the Bible tells me so;
Little ones to him belong –
They are weak, but he is strong.

Anna B. Warner (1827-1915)

Dear God,
Thank you that – with you –
I'm never alone.
Amen.

Jesus, friend of little children,
Be a friend to me;
Take my hand and ever keep me,
Close to thee.

Walter J. Mathams (1851-1931)

God made the sun,
And God made the trees,
God made the mountains,
And God made me.

Thank you, God,
For the sun and the trees,
For making the mountains,
And for making me.

Dear Lord Jesus,
Thank you for loving me.
I love you too.
Amen.

Give me love in my heart, Lord Jesus:
Love for you
Love for those around me
And love for everyone
I find difficult to like.

Dear Lord Jesus,
When you were a child living on earth,
you always obeyed your parents.
Please help me to do the same.
Thank you.

Dear Lord Jesus
I'm glad that
even if I forget about you,
You will never forget me.

Father God,
Knowing that you love me
makes me feel all warm and happy inside.
Thank you.

Two little eyes to look to God;
Two little ears to hear his word;
Two little feet to walk in his ways;
Two little lips to sing his praise;
Two little hands to do his will
And one little heart to love him still.

The Lord is my shepherd;
I have everything I need.
He lets me rest in fields
   of green grass
and leads me to quiet pools
   of fresh water.

Psalm 23

Give me joy in my heart,
Keep me praising,
Give me joy in my heart, I pray.
Give me joy in my heart,
Keep me praising –
Keep me praising
Till the break of day.

God be in my head
And in my understanding;
God be in my eyes,
And in my looking;
God be in my mouth
And in my speaking;
God be in my heart
And in my thinking.

Sarum Primer (1527)

Jesus Our Friend

Jesus bids us shine
With a pure, clear light,
Like a little candle
Burning in the night;
In this world of darkness,
So we must shine,
You in your small corner,
And I in mine.

Anonymous

Christ be with me
Christ within me
Christ behind me
Christ before me
Christ beside me
Christ to win me
Christ to comfort
Christ to guide

St Patrick (389-461)

Lord Jesus,
Help me be strong and brave.
Take my fear away.
Amen.

Lord Jesus Christ
Fill us with your love
That we may count nothing
Too small to do for you;
Nothing too much to give,
And nothing to hard to bear.

Ignatius Loyola (1491-1556)

Jesus, you have a loving heart.
Help mine be loving too.
Jesus, you have gentle hands.
Help mine be gentle too.
Amen.

All the People
I Love

God bless all those that I love;
God bless all those that love me;
God bless all those that love those that I love,
And all those who love those that love me.

From an old New England sampler

Lord Jesus,
Thank you for grandma and grandad.
Please look after them as they
  grow older.
Amen.

Dear God,
Thank you so much for my family.
Please look after all the lonely children
  everywhere, Lord.
Amen.

Lord Jesus
Please make my friend well.
Help the doctors and nurses
make her better.
Amen.

Bless this house O Lord we pray;
Make it safe by night and day;
Bless these walls so firm and stout,
Keeping want and trouble out:
Bless the roof and chimneys tall,
Let thy peace lie over all;
Bless this door, that it may prove
ever open to joy and love.

For health and food,
For love and friends,
For everything your goodness sends,
Father in Heaven, we thank you.
Amen.

Father God,
Thank you for my family –
not just those who live with us,
but grandparents, uncles, aunts and cousins.
Please be with all of them today.
Amen.

Dear God
Please love me,
Take care of me,
Bless me.

Please love my sister,
Take care of her,
Bless her.

Please love my brother,
Take care of him,
Bless him.
Amen.

Dear God,
Thank you that I have a nice home.
Not everyone does.
Thank you that I have family around me.
Not everyone does.
Thank you that I have toys and games.
Not everyone does.
Please look after all the children who go
  without.
Amen.

Lord Jesus
My friend moved away last week.
I miss her and she misses me.
Help us both to find new friends
So that we stop feeling sad.
Amen.

God let our home be friendly,
With open doors to all
Who come for food and shelter,
Or just to pay a call.

Sorry!

Dear God,
We're sorry for doing wrong things.
Please forgive us.
And help us forgive people
  who are unkind to us.
Amen.

God, you are great.
You made the world – and it's good.
Thank you for making it so beautiful.
We're sorry we've spoilt it.
Amen.

Lord,
I'm sorry for my bad mood today.
I'm glad that, whether I'm good or bad,
You love me anyway.

Dear God,
I did something wrong today.
You know what it was, God.
I'm sorry.
Please forgive me.
Thank you, God.

For the things that I've done wrong
Things that I remember long,
Hurting friends and those I love –
I am very sorry, God

All things bright and beautiful

All things bright and beautiful,
All creatures great and small,
All things wise and wonderful
The Lord God made them all.

He gave us eyes to see them,
And lips that we might tell,
How great is God Almighty,
Who has made all things well.

Mrs C. F. Alexander (1818-95)

For air and sunshine, pure and sweet,
We thank our heavenly father;
For grass that grows beneath our feet,
We thank our heavenly father.

Dear Father, hear and bless
Your beasts and singing birds;
And guard with tenderness
Small things that have no words.

Anonymous

Dear Lord,
Today we went to the zoo.
We saw lots of animals you made.
Giant elephants, teeny lizards,
Chattering monkeys, gentle deer,
Waddling penguins, roaring lions.
You made them all, God,
Big and small.

Thank you God for rain
and beautiful rainbows.
Thank you for letting us
splash in the puddles.

God, who made the earth,
The air, the sky, the sea,
Who gave the light its birth
Careth for me.

God, who made the grass,
The flower, the fruit, the tree,
The day and night to pass,
Careth for me.

God, who made all things,
On earth, in air, in sea,
Who changing seasons brings,
Careth for me

Sarah Betts Rhodes (c. 1870)

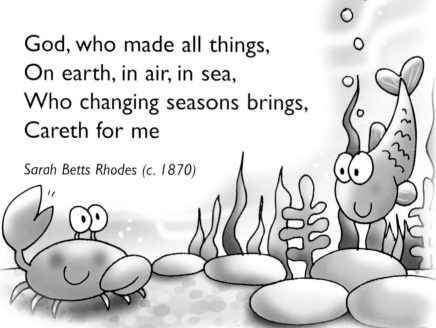

Lord
Thank you that we can sing to you.
Because music is such fun,
and we sing such great songs.
Amen.

Thank you for spring,
When lambs are born
And flowers bloom.

Thank you for long, hot summer days,
When we can play outside
And enjoy the sunshine.

Thank you for autumn,
When fruit is ripe for picking
And golden leaves tumble from trees.

And thank you for winter,
With its ice and snow.

Now thank we all our God
With hearts and hands and voices;
Such wonders he has done
In him his world rejoices.

Martin Rinkart (1586-1649)

Extra-special Days

Christmas

Away in a manger
No crib for a bed,
The little Lord Jesus
Laid down his sweet head.

The stars in the bright sky
Look down where he lay
The little Lord Jesus
Asleep in the hay.

Martin Luther

What can I give him,
Poor as I am?
If I were a shepherd,
I would bring a lamb;
If I were a wise man,
I would do my part;
Yet what I can I give him?
Give my heart.

Christina Rosetti (1830-94)

Thank you, Father God,
for giving us your son, baby Jesus.

Lord Jesus,
Wise men journeyed for miles to bring you
 the first Christmas presents.
Help us remember the love that comes with
 each present we open.
Amen.

May Christmas morning make us happy
  to be your children
And Christmas evening bring us to our
  beds with grateful thoughts,
Forgiving and forgiven,
For Jesus' sake,
Amen.

Robert Louis Stevenson (1850-94)

Easter

There is a green hill far away
Outside a city wall
Where the dear Lord was crucified
Who died to save us all.

Mrs C. F. Alexander

Jesus Christ is risen today.
Alleluia

Harvest

All good gifts around us
Are sent from heaven above.
Then thank the Lord,
O thank the Lord,
For all his love.

Matthias Claudius (1740-1815)
Translated by Jane Montgomery Campbell (1817-78)

First the seed
And then the grain;
Thank you, God,
For sun and rain.

Thank you, God,
For all your care;
Help us all
To share and share.

Birthdays

Thank you, Lord,
for people and parties,
For presents and cards,
for cakes and candles.
Thank you for birthdays, Lord.

Today it's my birthday!
Please give me a happy day –
and all the other children born today.

Holidays

Thank you, God, for holidays –
For summer clothes and summer play –
And sunny summer days.

Thank you,
thank you,
thank you!

For blue of stream and blue of sky,
Father, we thank you.
For pleasant shade of branches high,
Father we thank you.
For fragrant air and cooling breeze,
For beauty of the flowering trees,
Father in heaven, we thank you.

Ralph Waldo Emerson (1803-82)

For food and clothes and toys and such,
We thank you, Lord, so very much.
Amen.

God made the sun,
And God made the trees.
God made the flowers,
And God made the bees.

Thank you, God, for the sun
And the trees.
For wonderful flowers
And buzzing bees.

For the sounds I hear
And the sights I see,
But most of all,
Thank you for making me!

Thank you for:

Sun
Rain
Beautiful flowers
Cats
Tall trees
Twisting rivers
Wriggly, wiggly worms
Bright leaves
Orangey sunset
Dogs
Peacocks
Daffodils
For food, for friends,
For all God sends.
We give our thanks
to you.
Amen.

Sweet Dreams

Dear God,
I love bathtime.
I make lots and lots of bubbles.
I pretend I'm swimming in the sea.
It's such fun.
Thank you for my bathtime.

Hello God!
It's me!
What a great day it's been.
Did you see everything I did today?
Of course –
Because you're God!
Thanks for being with me.
Amen.

Father God,
When dad turns off the light,
please be with me.
Help me to get to sleep,
and please give me good dreams.
Amen.

Hello God
Did you hear me laughing today?
It was so funny.
Thank you for giving us so much fun.

Hello God!
I saw so many people today.
*My best friend.
*My teacher.
*My brother and sister.
*The lady next door.
Thanks for all the great people in my day.
Amen.

Dear God
I'm sorry I was naughty today.
Please help me to be nice to
My parents tomorrow.
And kind to my sister.
Amen.

'Taps'

Day is done.
Gone the sun,
From the lake,
From the hills,
From the sky.
All is well,
safely rest.
God is near.

Anonymous

Thank you Father, *Thank you Father*,
For this day, *For this day*,
And for all our family,
And for all our family,
Thank you Lord, *Thank you Lord*.

To the tune of "Frère Jacques"

Bless us in the morning,
Bless us through the day,
Bless us as we go to sleep,
And keep us safe, we pray.

Lord Jesus
Thank you for everything good that
  happened today:
For keeping me safe and well.
For fun with friends,
For what I learned,
For those I love.
Help me to sleep safely tonight.
Amen.

Now the light has gone away;
Jesus, listen while I pray.
Asking you to watch and keep
And to send me quiet sleep.

Jesus, tender Shepherd, hear me:
Bless your little lamb tonight;
Through the darkness please be near me,
Keep me safe till morning light.

All this day your hand has led me,
And I thank you for your care;
You have warmed me, clothed and fed me;
Listen to my evening prayer.

Mary L. Duncan (1814-40)

I see the moon,
And the moon sees me:
God bless the moon,
And God bless me.

Traditional

Now that I lie down to sleep,
I ask you, Lord, your child to keep.
Your love be with me through the night,
And wake me in the morning light.

Traditional

God watches over us all the day,
At home, at school at play;
And when the sun has left the skies,
He watches with a million eyes.

Gabriel Setoun (Thomas Nicoll Hepburn) (1861-1930)

Dear Lord Jesus,
As a hen covers her chicks with her wings
To keep them safe,
Protect us this dark night
Under your golden wings.

Prayer from India

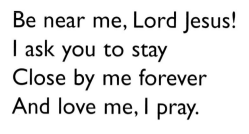

Be near me, Lord Jesus!
I ask you to stay
Close by me forever
And love me, I pray.

Bless all the dear children
In your tender care
And take us to heaven
To live with you there.

Martin Luther

Soft moonbeams light the garden,
The sky is starry bright,
Dear Father up in heaven,
Please bless us all tonight.

While We Sleep

I go to bed
And sleep in peace,
For you, Lord, keep me safe.

From Psalm 4

The moon shines bright,
The stars give light
Before the break of day.

God bless you all,
Both great and small,
And send a joyful day.

Traditional

Loving shepherd of your sheep,
Keep your lamb, in safety keep;
Nothing can your power withstand
None can take me from your hand.

Jane Eliza Leeson (1807-82)

Dear God,

Please look after me at bedtime.

Sometimes I wake up in the middle of the night and feel a bit scared.

Help me to remember that you are always with me.

Then I won't need to be afraid.

As night-time comes creeping,
And children are sleeping,
God watches us, deep through the night.

So hush now, no peeping,
For God will be keeping
Us safe, till the new morning's light.

Lord, keep us safe tonight,
Protect us from all fears.
May angels guard us while we sleep
Till morning light appears.

John Leland (1754-1841)

Hello God
I'm thinking about tomorrow.
It's a new day.
Help me do something special
And something kind

When the sun has said goodbye
And little stars shine in the sky
You're still with me, not far above,
Right in my heart, for you are love.

Matthew, Mark, Luke and John,
Bless the bed that I lie on.
Four corners to my bed
Four angels round are spread.

Traditional

Goodnight! Goodnight!
Far flies the light;
But still God's love,
Shall flame above,
Making all bright.
Good Night!
Good Night!

Victor Hugo